JUST US

BY Rev. Russell Young

When i am writing this book, i am wondering how many Americans actually know what

their God given, United States of America, rights are? How many Americans know that the bill

of rights, which us veterans fought for, are there for their protection...

Do you, America, know what your rights are? do you know how many of your rights have

changed over the last 20 years? or even the last 40 years?

Do you, America, know what you are doing when it comes to the law?

Sometimes, the best way to protect yourself is to have knowledge. Knowledge is the key

to keeping yourself out of trouble and out of harms way.

Some people, or most, have heard or seen this saying:

Well?....

Can you see where i am coming from? Ask yourself this question: do i speak evil, do i

hear evil, or do i see evil? If you answered any of these questions, you need to examine

yourself... Evil comes in many ways...remember this...

Some people have to get arrested to wake themselves up...this is a sad state when you

have to go through this...they have to get arrested just to shake themselves awake to the realities

of the (Justice) system. Because of what I believe in I am going to pronounce Justice as just us...

ok?

In this book i am going to "advise" you on (some) of the ways that you can "protect"

yourself when you are, or have been, arrested.

BEFORE WE BEGIN;

I have written a book called "Homeless American Veteran" which tells you of some of

the HELL I have been through. I want to assure you that while this book may contain certain forms you have to do when you have been arrested, IN NO WAY WILL I LIE TO YOU and show you a wrong way to do things.

QUALIFICATIONS:

To show you that I know what I am doing, here are my qualifications:

(A): I served 6 years in the United States Navy, and with that 3 wars;

(B): I am an ordained minister;

(C): I served a total of almost 18 years in prison or lockup. The longest was 6 years. I have also been convicted, 3 times, of crimes to which I did not do. (Please read Homeless American Veteran)

(D): During my 18 years of being locked up, 16 years of that have been studying law. Both criminal and civil law.

(AGAIN: I WILL ALWAYS TELL YOU THE TRUTH, BECAUSE IF I DO NOT KNOW ANYTHING, I ASK, OR I GO LOOK IT UP). You can look up all that I say on www.findlaw. com OK?

OK here we go.

you ready?

(Sit-rep, or if you were not in the military, situation report):

Some police officers hand cuffed you and told you, you were under arrest,

OK, now what?

(1): Did you ask what you were being ***arrested for?*** And what did they say?;

If not then:

(2): Did you say, " I want to call my lawyer", or say "I want a lawyer"?

Do you have a lawyer on retainer? If you do have a lawyer on

retainer then you do not need this book, unless you are like me and do not trust them.....If you

trust your lawyer to give you good representation then please give this book to someone who do

not have that trust in their lawyer...

(3): If you do not have a lawyer on retainer, then you need this book. Ok. You got

arrested, got some county jewelry put on you, (that is handcuffs), and you got sent to the county

jail, or where ever they put you. OK, welcome to the system. Now you are going to see what it is

like to be me. PARTLY.

(4): You were arrested. Did you get your Miranda rights said to you?

OK what are my Miranda rights?

According to findlaw.com (Miranda rights: The famous Miranda rights for criminal

suspects, often heard recited in movies or on t.v., came from the landmark U.S. supreme court

case of Miranda v. Arizona and are based on the 5th amendment. The ruling in Miranda and

subsequent cases provide criminal suspects with a number of rights when being question by law

enforcement officers. The officers (must) tell you 4 things before questioning you. (A): You have

the right to remain silent; (B): Anything you say can and will be used against you in a court of

law; (C): You have the right to an attorney; (D): If you can not afford an attorney, one will be

appointed to you.)

Now definition of *MUST:* the definition of must is in the same category as

shall: Shall: As used in statutes and similar instruments, this word is generally imperative or

mandatory but it may be construed as merely permissive or directing, as equivalent to may or must, to carry out the legislative intention and in cases where no right or benefit to any one depends on its being taken in the imperative sense, and where no public or private right is impaired by it's interpretation in the other sense. Otherwise defined as (They do not have to say it to you and good luck proving it).

WOW a lot huh? You have not even touched the surface yet. Oh yea I forgot one more definition: sorry!!!!

Right: Right, (a.k.a. common right), is a term applied to rights, privileges, and immunities appertaining to and enjoyed by all citizens, equally and in common, which have their foundation in common law.

Did you know that as a U.S. citizen you were born with or naturalized with many rights? at the end of this book I will show you your U.S. constitutional rights that you S H A L L know. You need to know them. SERIOUSLY!!!

(5): Now what if the police fail to advise me of my Miranda rights? Well then, anything you have stated to them is (involuntary) and can NOT be used against you in a court of law; And anything that you have said will be thrown out of court, (if you are lucky enough to have them say they did not read you your rights).

Now comes the banger: Can YOU prove, (beyond a reasonable doubt), that the officer(s) stated or read you your Miranda rights?

Definition according to findlaw.com: (**Beyond reasonable doubt**- Reasonable doubt could be defined as ones thoughts of an issue, or statement, in doubt as to the truth of the issue or statement. If one of the jury personnel has doubt as to the truthfulness of a witness then reasonable doubt is presumed. It is that state of the case which after the entire comparison and consideration of all the evidence, leaves the minds of the jurors in that condition that they can not say they feel an abiding conviction to a moral certainty of the truth of the charge. Other words, in this case, members of the jury can not find enough evidence to convict). Remember the burden of proof is upon the prosecutor. You are innocent until proven guilty, but in these days you are

guilty until you are proven innocent....)

So you can not prove that your Miranda rights were said or read to you. Still; The prosecution district attorney [*SHALL*] prove *BEYOND A REASONABLE DOUBT* you did the crime.

Definition of *CRIME*- (*A crime is an act committed or omitted in violation of a public law, either forbidding or commanding it..); Definition of PUBLIC LAW-(Pertaining to laws of a city, county, state, nation or whole community. Public laws differ when you are in different cities, townships, villages, county's and states. Check them where you are.)*

(6): Now that they have you, can you post a bond?

If not keep reading. If so keep reading anyway.

If you can afford a bond, get out and stay clean. DO NOT FUCK UP WHILE ON BOND. YOUR ASS WILL BE DONE FOR.....

You are out on bond, good, go look up law and help your lawyer do his/her job. ASK QUESTIONS;

THE MOST STUPID QUESTION IN THE WORLD IS?

ONE NOT ASKED!!!!!

RIGHT?

Remember what I stated before? The more you know the better off you are. If you know the law then you know how to protect yourself.

(7): If you are not out on bond, and are reading this book while you are locked up, LISTEN UP!!!!!!

GO TO THE LAW LIBRARY AS MUCH AS YOU CAN. Do a request form... I.R.F. (Inmate request form) as they call it in most county jails; to go to the law library....and look up your superior court/supreme court laws..and, or, rules.....(NOTE: READ THESE AND KNOW THEM INSIDE AND OUT)....If you are denied, for any reason, keep the request form and file a grievance with the sheriff. A letter to the sheriff is not illegal and if you are not given a response you can file a lawsuit for denial of access to the court. Remember this:

(A): The sheriff of the county where you are locked up has absolute control of the county jail. The city jail you can send a grievance to the judge..

(B): Now both the sheriff and the Judge will check and see if you are represented by counsel. If you are represented by counsel then they will say to you that if you have questions regarding your case you need to ask your lawyer/counsel. Then you tell the sheriff/Judge that you do not trust the counsel to properly represent you and that you have no funds to do anything about it....but you would like to have access to the law library as is permitted in the constitution of the United States of America...

(C): That's when you KEEP ALL PAPERWORK TO SHOW JUST CAUSE FOR A LAWSUIT FOR DENIAL OF ACCESS TO THE COURT. YOU CAN STATE THE OBVIOUS FACT THAT YOU DO NOT TRUST YOUR LAWYER/COUNSEL AND YOU NEED TO LOOK UP THE LAW YOURSELF. You need to state that the law states that you have the RIGHT to access to the court which also implies the RIGHT to use the law library for research into your case...

(D): If you think you can you can appear Pro Se in your case...but remember this...You have to have knowledge of the laws of your county and your state and also have knowledge of how the court system works... ALSO remember this: If the law library is incomplete: does not have state and

federal laws and codes.... then you can ask to have access to the law library that does.... you can file suit for this...esp. an incomplete law library is against the law....... You must know what you are doing. Do not give up and never trust your lawyer. Look things up for your self...

Abraham Lincoln quoted: " I am a firm believer in the people. If given the [TRUTH], they can be depended upon to meet any national crises. The great point is to bring them the real facts"

(8): Now you go in front of the Judge for the first time;

(A): If you are going to have counsel represent you, you need to stop reading this book and start looking things up for your own safety. Remember, if you did not pay for your lawyer, then that lawyer works with and for the state. DO NOT LET THEM TELL YOU DIFFERENT...I CAN PROVE THEY DO;

Here's the proof. Ask your court appointed lawyer who pays him/her to be there. Are they doing this Pro Bono? They will probably tell you some bullshit so take care of your self.. [Pro Bono- Of their own resources. Without pay or compensation.]

Your lawyer is paid a certain amount to represent you in court. Depending on your case; (whether you are a high profile case or not) your lawyer gets about $150-$300 per visit. Payed by the state. Mine made $250/visit in Washington State; If the lawyer is paid by the state, then they will do what the state attorney tells them to do... Do you know what I mean now??

Now comes the hardest part of defending yourself. Do you trust your lawyer with your life?? Remember it is [YOUR] life that is on trial here not your lawyers...Lawyers do not care for your feelings, thoughts, or emotions. To them you are just a case number with a $$ sign on it. You are only worth money to them, not anything else.

(9): Have you asked for discovery evidence? Did your lawyer ask for it? Usually there is a form given to the lawyers about what evidence can be brought forth to the jury trial; But remember, the case Brady vs. Maryland? Under Brady, you have the **RIGHT** to have favorable evidence given to *YOU*, not your lawyer. If the prosecution does not turn over favorable evidence to *YOU* they are in violation of Brady.

[Brady vs. Maryland- 373 US 83 (syllabus (a)): Suppression by the prosecution of evidence favorable to an accused who has requested it violates due process, where the evidence is material either to guilt, or to punishment, irrespective of good faith or bad faith of the prosecution.]
Also relying on Mooney vs. Holohan, 294 U.S. 103, 294 US 112, where the court ruled on what nondisclosure by a prosecutor violates due process....

Remember people, the more that you know, the better off you will be. Do your legwork on your own. Compare it to your lawyers work. If that is not up to speed then keep track of it.

If your lawyer suppresses evidence that he/she gives no knowledge of but has in their possession, then you have a case of ineffective assistance of counsel. (WOW a lot huh?) Well:

legalmatch.com states in for ineffective assistance of counsel: the Supreme Court defined ineffective assistance of counsel, in the landmark case- Strickland vs. Washington (1984). The court held that an attorneys assistance is ineffective if it "so undermined the functioning of the adverse process that the trial can not be relied upon as having produced a just result.

Now, how do you prove that your counsel, lawyer, was ineffective (did not do their hob properly)? You can look up on Strickland vs. Maryland because that is federal law...

(Now before I go on, I am going to tell you the difference between Federal Law and State law. Federal law comes from the "Higher Courts" and are deemed the Supreme Law of the land. By definition, the U.S. Constitution is considered the "Supreme Law of the land". This means that when ever there is a conflict between state and federal laws, the federal law will take Precedence, under what is known as the "Supremacy Clause".)

State judges are mandated by law to uphold the Federal laws under the constitution. Now state laws are laws by which EACH STATE is held responsible for. Do you realize that each time the legislatures go into their jobs, that laws change? Laws, both Federal, and State, do change from time to time. State laws are those in which states, like New York, have passed to which the state preforms upon. Did you know that each state has their own constitution ? Look it up and keep that in your head.

Remember that when you are going through this, many things can happen. There are many venues and paths to which your case can go.

To show ineffective assistance of counsel, the defendant (YOU), must show that their attorney's performance was (deficient) because of the attorneys making such serious mistakes. Then the defendant must show that the attorney's mistakes prejudiced the defendants case. Prejudice in a case must be defined in the lawsuit or the appeal, and you have to show that it under minded the trial courts decision, and the decision would have been different, had the attorney not made those mistakes...

WOW HUH?   YOU STUMPED YET?   DONT WORRY IT ONLY GETS BETTER.....

NOTE: You can claim ineffective assistance of counsel on appeal. Not during your trial, unless you can prove, beyond a reasonable doubt, that your attorney is "hiding something" from you. Remember that you have the RIGHT to reasonable representation. "Every defendant is entitled to a trial in which his interests are vigorously and conscientiously advocated by an able lawyer" Also, you can find ineffective assistance of counsel under the case of Gideon vs. Wainwright, 372 US 335 (1963); Chapman vs. California, 386 US 18, 23 (1967). Yes these cases are old, but see the US in between the numbers?, these are FEDERAL case law and judges tend to listen to FEDERAL LAW for the purpose of keeping their Jobs....

Can you file a suit against your court appointed lawyer for ineffective assistance of counsel?, *__yes, as long as you can prove it.__* You can also sue the prosecution and the judge. Its just hard as hell to do that because prosecutors and judges have immunities to which you have to find a loop hole around....keep reading...keep your knowledge growing...

HINT: Judges and prosecutors take an oath or affirmation to support and defend the constitution of their respective states and Federal Constitution. And so does the prosecution. Lawyers have their own set of rules that they have to abide by...look those up....your case will be better handled if you know the LAWYERS CREED...hint hint hint....

Remember case law has to be positive. Case law is court cases that they have written into the law books so that idiots like me can read them to see what that particular case involved and how the judge rules....

Here's you a sample of the Lawyers Oath that your Lawyer has to abide by:

(1): I do solemnly swear, (or affirm);

(2): I will support the constitution of the united states and the constitution of the state of_____;

(3): I will maintain the respect due to courts of justices and judicial officers;

(4): I will not counsel or maintain any suit or proceeding which SHALL appear to me to be unjust, nor any defense except such as I believe to be honestly debatable under the law of the land;

(5): I will employ for the purposes of maintaining the causes confided to me such means only as are consistent with truth and honor, and will never seek to mislead the judge or jury by any artifice or false statement of fact or law;

(6): I will maintain the confidence and preserve inviolate the secrets of my client and will accept no compensation in connection with my clients business except with my clients knowledge and approval;

(7): I will abstain from all offensive personality, and advance no fact prejudicial to the honor or reputation of a party or witness, unless required by the justice of the cause with which I am charged.

(8): I will never reject, from any consideration personal to myself, the cause of the defenseless or oppressed, or delay any cause for lucre or malice;

(9): I will in all other respects, conduct myself personally and professionally in conformity with the high standards of conduct imposed upon members of the BAR as conditions for the privilege to practice law in this case and state.

The judges also have an oath and it goes something like this:

[I,_____, do solemnly swear (or affirm) that I will administer justice without respect to persons, and do [equal right] to the poor and to the rich, and

that I will faithfully and impartially discharge and perform all the duties incumbent upon me
as_____under the constitution and laws of the United States. So help me God..]

Remember , you have just started the process of defending yourself in this world of corruption..

(10): Now that you are going to trial; (Hey you! YOU ARE GOING TO TRIAL, ARE YOU?) If you plead guilty then you have just LOST.

NEVER PLEAD GUILTY

EVER

Trust me, that is the worst mistake in the world to do. I have done it some times and it has taken my life away....Now I have no life and I am a prisoner in my own home....because of pleading guilty...and have ruined my life, liberty, and happiness.

If you are one of those who want to plead GUILTY, then here's a couple of things you should know:

(1): PLEA NO CONTEST, OR NOLO CONTENDERE, because this is stating to the Judge that you are guilty of the crime but do not agree with the circumstances of or the evidence in which can get you a guilty verdict in trial. If you have not plead this and you have plead guilty, hang up your hat, you are done...unless you come up with new evidence with which you can make a Motion to reverse or remove the guilty plea....

(2): Sign everything with (S.U.D.)- Signed under duress. When you do this it is telling everyone that you DO NOT UNDERSTAND THE LAWS AND THE PROCESS TO WHICH THIS CASE IS GOING.... and you can also state on the plea of guilty that the D.A. Or prosecuting attorney, and your lawyer has stated that" you will do more time if you don't sign a guilty plea". Otherwise also called " Not of free will" You are signing under duress because you are not of free willing doing this....You need to prove hostility between you and the D.A. Like their track record of convictions by plea agreements vs. trial court....hint hint hint....

I know how it is. You are sitting in county jail, locked up for months on end trying to fight your case. You are basically in limbo from your life. You want to go free. Want to go home. I know how you feel. I was in county lockup for more than a year in Harris County, Houston Texas. ....

Now you are going to trial. Do you know that you have a speedy trial right? (Here we go again, right?)

wikipedia.org states "the speedy trial clause of the 6th Amendment to the US Constitution provides that "[I]n all criminal prosecutions, the accused ***SHALL*** enjoy the right to a speedy.....trial...." The Clause protects the defendant from delay between the presentation of the indictment or similar charging instrument and the beginning of trial"

YOU MUST AND SHALL KNOW THE SPPEDY TRIAL LAWS IN YOUR STATE. Like in Cowlitz County, Washington State, it is 60 days, then they have to bring you to trial. In New York its 6 months. In Houston Texas, it can take up to a year. Get the D.A. Or prosecuting attorney to acknowledge that you know you have the right to a speedy trial...

OK NOW WHAT?

GOOD QUESTION !

DO YOU KNOW WHAT A TRIAL BY JURY IS?

In the United States, the 6th Amendment states, "In all criminal prosecutions, the accused

SHALL enjoy the right to a speedy and public trial, by an impartial jury of the state and district wherein

the crime shall have been committed".

REMEMBER that once you have a jury trial, the jurors have the power now. They can, if they

want, in the middle of trial, can state that they find you not guilty. In Sparf et. al. vs. U.S. 156 U.S. 51

(1895): "It is our deep and settled conviction, confirmed by a re-examination of the authorities that the

jury, upon the general issue of guilty or not guilty in a criminal case, have the right as well as the power

to decide, according to their own judgment and consciences, all questions, whether of law or of fact

involved in that issue". The jury has the power now. Not the judge.

WOW! HOLD ON A MINUTE:

Did you get arrested with a grand jury indictment? Or did you get

arrested by a probable cause warrant? Or did the police just handcuff you and take you to jail?

[A grand jury indictment is a formal written charge issued by a grand jury in a criminal case.

Typically, the jury is charged with determining whether enough evidence exists to charge a suspect with

a criminal offense. But remember, You are not there, nor are you represented by counsel. This is an arm (helper) of the prosecution and only the prosecution.

Is that legal? YES AND NO.

YES- because it is part of the prosecutors arm, and NO- because you are not represented. No one has won, on appeal, on that issue though.

Remember you do not have to do anything. Except keep your ass safe. The prosecution has to

prove, **_BEYOND A REASONABLE DOUBT,_** you did the crime. And they have to take you to trial before your speedy trial date, or face a dismissal (with prejudice)

Remember: When a judgment is rendered WITH PREJUDICE , there is no further action that can be brought forth. When it is rendered WITHOUT PREDJUDICE, there is further action you can bring forth...

Now you are going to trial, are you ready? Is your attorney ready? Is all evidence there? What witnesses is the DA/prosecution/state bringing forth? Who are your attorneys going to call as a witness for you? Have you got all the BRADY evidence? Remember if you do not have all the evidence that the prosecution has, and no one will let you look at the record, then you must record this. A case can be thrown out of court because of [LACK OF EVIDENCE]. This is why you should always have an evidentiary hearing.... Remember that a Motion to Dismiss is necessary when YOU feel that someone is hiding something from you. You can do a Motion to Dismiss yourself...just get the form from any attorney or the court....really easy....just remember to put down why you think this case should be dismissed and what evidence is lacking...

Now remember, what I have written is what I have experienced in my case, and some of this you can actually use in your case....Just be careful of what you do in your case, because you are playing with YOUR LIFE, YOUR KIDS LIVES, YOUR FAMILYS LIVES.....

Please remember, trust no one and look for yourself the knowledge and information you need to keep you safe in the courtroom....keep your faith..... and most of all.......

<u>*NEVER PLEAD GUILTY.....*</u>

PLEASE

The following is the U.S. Constitution in which you should know....read it...please!!!!

We the People of the United States, in Order to form a more perfect Union, establish Justice, insure domestic Tranquility, provide for the common defense, promote the general Welfare, and secure the Blessings of Liberty to ourselves and our Posterity, do ordain and establish this Constitution for the United States of America.

Article I

Section 1

All legislative Powers herein granted shall be vested in a Congress of

the United States, which shall consist of a Senate and House of

Representatives.

Section 2

1: The House of Representatives shall be composed of Members chosen every second Year by the People of the several States, and the Electors in each State shall have the Qualifications requisite for Electors of the most numerous Branch of the State Legislature.

2: No Person shall be a Representative who shall not have attained to the Age of twenty five Years, and been seven Years a Citizen of the United States, **and who shall not, when elected, be an Inhabitant of that State in which he shall be chosen.**

3: Representatives and direct Taxes shall be apportioned among the several States which may be included within this Union, according to their respective Numbers, which shall be determined by adding to the whole Number of free Persons, including those bound to Service for a Term of Years, and excluding Indians not taxed, three fifths of all other Persons. The actual Enumeration shall be made within three Years after the first Meeting of the Congress of the United States, and within every subsequent Term of ten Years, in such Manner as they shall by Law direct. The Number of Representatives shall not exceed one for every thirty Thousand, but each State shall have at Least one Representative; and until such enumeration shall be made, the State of

New Hampshire shall be entitled to cause three, Massachusetts eight, Rhodes-Island and Providence Plantations one, Connecticut five, New-York six, New Jersey four, Pennsylvania eight, Delaware one, Maryland six, Virginia ten, North Carolina five, South Carolina five, and Georgia three.

4: When vacancies happen in the Representation from any State, the Executive Authority thereof shall issue Writs of Election to fill such Vacancies.

5: The House of Representatives shall cause their Speaker and other Officers; and shall have the sole Power of Impeachment.

Section 3

1: The Senate of the United States shall be composed of two Senators from each State, chosen by the Legislature thereof, for six years; and each Senator shall have one Vote.

2: Immediately after they shall be assembled in Consequence of the first Election, they shall be divided as equally as may be into three Classes. The Seats of the Senators of the first Class shall be vacated at the Expiration of the second Year, of the second Class at the Expiration of the fourth Year, and of the third Class at the Expiration of the sixth

Year, so that one third may be chosen every second Year; and if

Vacancies happen by Resignation, or otherwise, during the Recess of

the Legislature of any State, the Executive thereof may make

temporary Appointments until the next Meeting of the Legislature,

which shall then fill such Vacancies.

3: *No Person shall be a Senator who shall not have attained to the Age of thirty Years, and been nine Years a Citizen of the United States, and*

who shall not, when elected be an Inhabitant of that State for which he shall be chosen.

4: The Vice President of the United States shall be President of the

Senate, but shall have no Vote, unless they be equally divided.

5: The Senate shall cause their other Officers, and also a President pro

tempore, in the Absence of the Vice President, or when he shall exercise

the Office of President of the United States.

6: The Senate shall have the sole Power to try all Impeachment. When

sitting for that Purpose, they shall be on Oath or Affirmation. When

the President of the United States is tried, the Chief Justice shall

preside: And no Person shall be convicted without the Concurrence of

two thirds of the Members present.

7: Judgment in Cases of impeachment shall not extend further than to removal from Office, and disqualification to hold and enjoy any Office of honor, Trust or Profit under the United States: but the Party convicted shall nevertheless be liable and subject to Indictment, Trial, Judgment and Punishment, according to Law.

Section 4

1: The Times, Places and Manner of holding Elections for Senators and Representatives, shall be prescribed in each State by the Legislature thereof; but the Congress may at any time by Law make or alter such Regulations, except as to the Places of causing Senators.

2: The Congress shall assemble at least once in every Year, and such Meeting shall be on the first Monday in December,5 unless they shall by Law appoint a different Day.

Section 5

1: Each House shall be the Judge of the Elections, Returns and Qualifications of its own Members, and a Majority of each shall constitute a Quorum to do Business; but a smaller Number may adjourn from day to day, and may be authorized to compel the Attendance of absent Members, in such Manner, and under such Penalties as each House may provide.

2: Each House may determine the Rules of its Proceedings, punish its Members for disorderly Behavior, and, with the Concurrence of two thirds, expel a Member.

3: Each House shall keep a Journal of its Proceedings, and from time to time publish the same, excepting such Parts as may in their Judgment require Secrecy; and the Yeas and Nays of the Members of either House on any question shall, at the Desire of one fifth of those Present, be entered on the Journal.

4: Neither House, during the Session of Congress, shall, without the Consent of the other, adjourn for more than three days, nor to any other Place than that in which the two Houses shall be sitting.

Section 6

1: The Senators and Representatives shall receive a Compensation for their Services, to be ascertained by Law, and paid out of the Treasury of the United States.6 They shall in all Cases, except Treason, Felony and Breach of the Peace, be privileged from Arrest during their Attendance at the Session of their respective Houses, and in going to and returning from the same; and for any Speech or Debate in either House, they shall not be questioned in any other Place.

2: No Senator or Representative shall, during the Time for which he was elected, be appointed to any civil Office under the Authority of the United States, which shall have been created, or the Emoluments whereof shall have been increased during such time; and no Person holding any Office under the United States, shall be a Member of either House during his Continuance in Office.

Section 7

1: All Bills for raising Revenue shall originate in the House of

Representatives; but the Senate may propose or concur with Amendments as on other Bills.

2: Every Bill which shall have passed the House of Representatives and the Senate, shall, before it become a Law, be presented to the President of the United States; If he approve he shall sign it, but if not he shall return it, with his Objections to that House in which it shall have originated, who shall enter the Objections at large on their Journal, and proceed to reconsider it. If after such Reconsideration two thirds of that House shall agree to pass the Bill, it shall be sent, together with the Objections, to the other House, by which it shall likewise be reconsidered, and if approved by two thirds of that House, it shall become a Law. But in all such Cases the Votes of both Houses shall be determined by yeas and Nays, and the Names of the Persons voting for and against the Bill shall be entered on the Journal of each House respectively. If any Bill shall not be returned by the President within ten Days (Sundays excepted) after it shall have been presented to him, the Same shall be a Law, in like Manner as if he had signed it, unless the Congress by their Adjournment prevent its Return, in which Case it shall not be a Law.

3: Every Order, Resolution, or Vote to which the Concurrence of the Senate and House of Representatives may be necessary (except on a question of Adjournment) shall be presented to the President of the United States; and before the Same shall take Effect, shall be approved by him, or being disapproved by him, shall be re passed by two thirds of the Senate and House of Representatives, according to the Rules and Limitations prescribed in the Case of a Bill.

Section 8

1: The Congress shall have Power To lay and collect Taxes, Duties, Imposts and Excises, to pay the Debts and provide for the common Defense and general Welfare of the United States; but all Duties,

Imposts and Excises shall be uniform throughout the United States;

2: To borrow Money on the credit of the United States;

3: To regulate Commerce with foreign Nations, and among the several States, and with the Indian Tribes;

4: To establish an uniform Rule of Naturalization, and uniform Laws on the subject of Bankruptcies throughout the United States;

5: To coin Money, regulate the Value thereof, and of foreign Coin, and fix the Standard of Weights and Measures;

6: To provide for the Punishment of counterfeiting the Securities and current Coin of the United States;

7: To establish Post Offices and post Roads;

8: To promote the Progress of Science and useful Arts, by securing for limited Times to Authors and Inventors the exclusive Right to their respective Writings and Discoveries;

9: To constitute Tribunals inferior to the supreme Court;

10: To define and punish Piracies and Felonies committed on the high Seas, and Offenses against the Law of Nations;

11: To declare War, grant Letters of Marque and Reprisal, and make

Rules concerning Captures on Land and Water;

12: To raise and support Armies, but no Appropriation of Money to that Use shall be for a longer Term than two Years;

13: To provide and maintain a Navy;

14: To make Rules for the Government and Regulation of the land and naval Forces;

15: To provide for calling forth the Militia to execute the Laws of the Union, suppress Insurrections and repel Invasions; (this is a good one)

16: To provide for organizing, arming, and disciplining, the Militia, and

for governing such Part of them as may be employed in the Service of the United States, reserving to the States respectively, the Appointment of the Officers, and the Authority of training the Militia according to the discipline prescribed by Congress;

17: To exercise exclusive Legislation in all Cases whatsoever, over such District (not exceeding ten Miles square) as may, by Cession of particular States, and the Acceptance of Congress, become the Seat of the Government of the United States, and to exercise like Authority over all Places purchased by the Consent of the Legislature of the State in which the Same shall be, for the Erection of Forts, Magazines, Arsenals, dock-Yards, and other needful Buildings;

18: To make all Laws which shall be necessary and proper for carrying into Execution the foregoing Powers, and all other Powers vested by this Constitution in the Government of the United States, or in any Department or Officer thereof.

Section 9

1: The Migration or Importation of such Persons as any of the States now existing shall think proper to admit, shall not be prohibited by the Congress prior to the Year one thousand eight hundred and eight, but a Tax or duty may be imposed on such Importation, not exceeding ten dollars for each Person.

2: The Privilege of the Writ of Habeas Corpus [SHALL] not be suspended, unless when in Cases of Rebellion or Invasion the public Safety may require it.

3: No Bill of Attainder or ex post facto Law shall be passed.

4: No Capitation, or other direct, Tax shall be laid, unless in Proportion to the Census or Enumeration herein before directed to be taken.

5: No Tax or Duty shall be laid on Articles exported from any State.

6: No Preference shall be given by any Regulation of Commerce or Revenue to the Ports of one State over those of another: nor shall Vessels bound to, or from, one State, be obliged to enter, clear, or pay Duties in another.

7: No Money shall be drawn from the Treasury, but in Consequence of Appropriations made by Law; and a regular Statement and Account of the Receipts and Expenditures of all public Money shall be published from time to time.

8: No Title of Nobility shall be granted by the United States: And no Person holding any Office of Profit or Trust under them, shall, without the Consent of the Congress, accept of any present, Emolument, Office, or Title, of any kind whatever, from any King, Prince, or foreign State.

Section 10

1: No State shall enter into any Treaty, Alliance, or Confederation; grant Letters of Marque and Reprisal; coin Money; emit Bills of Credit; make any Thing but gold and silver Coin a Tender in Payment of Debts; pass any Bill of Attainder, ex post facto Law, or Law impairing the

Obligation of Contracts, or grant any Title of Nobility.

2: No State shall, without the Consent of the Congress, lay any Imposts or Duties on Imports or Exports, except what may be absolutely necessary for executing it's inspection Laws: and the net Produce of all Duties and Imposts, laid by any State on Imports or Exports, shall be for the Use of the Treasury of the United States; and all such Laws shall be subject to the Revision and Control of the Congress.

3: No State shall, without the Consent of Congress, lay any Duty of Tonnage, keep Troops, or Ships of War in time of Peace, enter into any Agreement or Compact with another State, or with a foreign Power, or engage in War, unless actually invaded, or in such imminent Danger as will not admit of delay.

Article II

Section 1

1: The executive Power shall be vested in a President of the United States of America. He shall hold his Office during the Term of four Years, and, together with the Vice President, chosen for the same Term, be elected, as follows

2: Each State shall appoint, in such Manner as the Legislature thereof may direct, a Number of Electors, equal to the whole Number of Senators and Representatives to which the State may be entitled in the Congress: but no Senator or Representative, or Person holding an Office of Trust or Profit under the United States, shall be appointed an Elector.

3: The Electors shall meet in their respective States, and vote by Ballot for two Persons, of whom one at least shall not be an Inhabitant of the same State with themselves. And they shall make a List of all the Persons voted for, and of the Number of Votes for each; which List they shall sign and certify, and transmit sealed to the Seat of the Government of the United States, directed to the President of the Senate. The President of the Senate shall, in the Presence of the Senate and House of Representatives, open all the Certificates, and the Votes shall then be counted. The Person having the greatest Number of Votes shall be the President, if such Number be a Majority of the whole Number of Electors appointed; and if there be more than one who have such Majority, and have an equal Number of Votes, then the House of Representatives shall immediately cause by Ballot one of them for President; and if no Person have a Majority, then from the five highest on the List the said House shall in like Manner cause the President. But in causing the President, the Votes shall be taken by States, the Representation from each State having one Vote; A quorum for this Purpose shall consist of a Member or Members from two thirds of the States, and a Majority of all the States shall be necessary to a Choice. In every Case, after the Choice of the President, the Person having the greatest Number of Votes of the Electors shall be the Vice President. But if there should remain two or more who have equal Votes, the Senate shall cause from them by Ballot the Vice President.8

4: The Congress may determine the Time of causing the Electors, and the Day on which they shall give their Votes; which Day shall be the same throughout the United States.

5: No Person except a natural born Citizen, or a Citizen of the United

States, at the time of the Adoption of this Constitution, shall be eligible to the Office of President; neither shall any Person be eligible to that Office who shall not have attained to the Age of thirty five Years, and been fourteen Years a Resident within the United States.

6: In Case of the Removal of the President from Office, or of his Death, Resignation, or Inability to discharge the Powers and Duties of the said Office, the Same shall devolve on the Vice President, and the Congress may by Law provide for the Case of Removal, Death, Resignation or Inability, both of the President and Vice President, declaring what Officer shall then act as President, and such Officer shall act accordingly, until the Disability be removed, or a President shall be elected.

7: The President shall, at stated Times, receive for his Services, a Compensation, which shall neither be increased nor diminished during the Period for which he shall have been elected, and he shall not receive within that Period any other Emolument from the United States, or any of them.

8: Before he enter on the Execution of his Office, he shall take the following Oath or Affirmation:--"I do solemnly swear (or affirm) that I will faithfully execute the Office of President of the United States, and will to the best of my Ability, preserve, protect and defend the Constitution of the United States."

Section 2

1: The President shall be Commander in Chief of the Army and Navy of the United States, and of the Militia of the several States, when called into the actual Service of the United States; he may require the Opinion, in writing, of the principal Officer in each of the executive Departments, upon any Subject relating to the Duties of their respective Offices, and he shall have Power to grant Reprieves and Pardons for Offenses against the United States, except in Cases of Impeachment.

2: He shall have Power, by and with the Advice and Consent of the Senate, to make Treaties, provided two thirds of the Senators present concur; and he shall nominate, and by and with the Advice and Consent of the Senate, shall appoint Ambassadors, other public Ministers and Consuls, Judges of the supreme Court, and all other Officers of the United States, whose Appointments are not herein otherwise provided for, and which shall be established by Law: but the Congress may by Law vest the Appointment of such inferior Officers, as they think proper, in the President alone, in the Courts of Law, or in the Heads of Departments.

3: The President shall have Power to fill up all Vacancies that may happen during the Recess of the Senate, by granting Commissions which shall expire at the End of their next Session.

Section 3

He shall from time to time give to the Congress Information of the State of the Union, and recommend to their Consideration such Measures as he shall judge necessary and expedient; he may, on extraordinary Occasions, convene both Houses, or either of them, and in Case of Disagreement between them, with Respect to the Time of Adjournment, he may adjourn them to such Time as he shall think proper; he shall receive Ambassadors and other public Ministers; he shall take Care that the Laws be faithfully executed, and shall Commission all the Officers of the United States.

Section 4

The President, Vice President and all civil Officers of the United States, shall be removed from Office on Impeachment for, and Conviction of, Treason, Bribery, or other high Crimes and Misdemeanors.

Article III

Section 1

The judicial Power of the United States, shall be vested in one supreme Court, and in such inferior Courts as the Congress may from time to time ordain and establish. The Judges, both of the supreme and inferior Courts, shall hold their Offices during good Behavior, and shall, at stated Times, receive for their Services, a Compensation, which shall not be diminished during their Continuance in Office.

Section 2

1: The judicial Power shall extend to all Cases, in Law and Equity, arising under this Constitution, the Laws of the United States, and Treaties made, or which shall be made, under their Authority;--to all Cases affecting Ambassadors, other public Ministers and Consuls;--to all Cases of admiralty and maritime Jurisdiction;--to Controversies to which the United States shall be a Party;--to Controversies between two or more States;--between a State and Citizens of another State; between Citizens of different States, --between Citizens of the same State claiming Lands under Grants of different States, and between a State, or the Citizens thereof, and foreign States, Citizens or Subjects.

2: In all Cases affecting Ambassadors, other public Ministers and Consuls, and those in which a State shall be Party, the supreme Court shall have original Jurisdiction. In all the other Cases before mentioned, the supreme

Court shall have appellate Jurisdiction, both as to Law and Fact, with such

Exceptions, and under such Regulations as the Congress shall make.

3: The Trial of all Crimes, except in Cases of Impeachment, shall be by Jury; and such Trial shall be held in the State where the said Crimes shall have been committed; but when not committed within any State, the Trial shall be at such Place or Places as the Congress may by Law have directed.

Section 3

1: Treason against the United States, shall consist only in levying War

against them, or in adhering to their Enemies, giving them Aid and Comfort.

No Person shall be convicted of Treason unless on the Testimony of two

Witnesses to the same overt Act, or on Confession in open Court.

2: The Congress shall have Power to declare the Punishment of Treason, but

no Attainder of Treason shall work Corruption of Blood, or Forfeiture except

during the Life of the Person attained.

Article IV

Section 1

Full Faith and Credit shall be given in each State to the public Acts,

Records, and judicial Proceedings of every other State. And the Congress

may by general Laws prescribe the Manner in which such Acts, Records and

Proceedings shall be proved, and the Effect thereof.

Section 2

1: The Citizens of each State shall be entitled to all Privileges and Immunities of Citizens in the several States.

2: A Person charged in any State with Treason, Felony, or other Crime, who shall flee from Justice, and be found in another State, shall on Demand of the executive Authority of the State from which he fled, be delivered up, to be removed to the State having Jurisdiction of the Crime.

3: No Person held to Service or Labor in one State, under the Laws thereof, escaping into another, shall, in Consequence of any Law or Regulation therein, be discharged from such Service or Labor, but shall be delivered up on Claim of the Party to whom such Service or Labor may be due.11

Section 3

1: New States may be admitted by the Congress into this Union; but no new State shall be formed or erected within the Jurisdiction of any other State; nor any State be formed by the Junction of two or more States, or Parts of States, without the Consent of the Legislatures of the States concerned as well as of the Congress.

2: The Congress shall have Power to dispose of and make all needful Rules and Regulations respecting the Territory or other Property belonging to the United States; and nothing in this Constitution shall be so construed as to Prejudice any Claims of the United States, or of any particular State.

Section 4

The United States shall guarantee to every State in this Union a Republican Form of Government, and shall protect each of them against Invasion; and on Application of the Legislature, or of the Executive (when the Legislature cannot be convened) against domestic Violence.

Article V

The Congress, whenever two thirds of both Houses shall deem it necessary, shall propose Amendments to this Constitution, or, on the Application of the Legislatures of two thirds of the several States, shall call a Convention for proposing Amendments, which, in either Case, shall be valid to all Intents and Purposes, as Part of this Constitution, when ratified by the Legislatures of three fourths of the several States, or by Conventions in three fourths thereof, as the one or the other Mode of Ratification may be proposed by the Congress; Provided that no Amendment which may be made prior to the Year One thousand eight hundred and eight shall in any Manner affect the first and fourth Clauses in the Ninth Section of the first Article; and that no State, without its Consent, shall be deprived of its equal Suffrage in the Senate.

Article VI

1: All Debts contracted and Engagements entered into, before the Adoption of this Constitution, shall be as valid against the United States under this Constitution, as under the Confederation.

2: This Constitution, and the Laws of the United States which shall be made in Pursuance thereof; and all Treaties made, or which shall be made, under the Authority of the United States, shall be the supreme Law of the Land; and the Judges in every State shall be bound thereby, any Thing in the Constitution or Laws of any State to the Contrary notwithstanding.

3: The Senators and Representatives before mentioned, and the Members of the several State Legislatures, and all executive and judicial Officers, both of the United States and of the several States, shall be bound by Oath or Affirmation, to support this Constitution; but no religious Test shall ever be required as a Qualification to any Office or public Trust under the United States.

Article VII

The Ratification of the Conventions of nine States, shall be sufficient for the Establishment of this Constitution between the States so ratifying the Same.

(The Preamble to The Bill of Rights)

Congress OF THE United States
begun and held at the City of New-York, on Wednesday the fourth of March, one thousand seven hundred and eighty nine.

THE Conventions of a number of the States, having at the time of their adopting the Constitution, expressed a desire, in order to prevent misconstruction or abuse of its powers, that further declaratory and restrictive clauses should be added: And as extending the ground of public confidence in the Government, will best ensure the beneficent ends of its institution.

RESOLVED by the Senate and House of Representatives of the United States of America, in Congress assembled, two thirds of both Houses concurring, that the following Articles be proposed to the Legislatures of the several States, as amendments to the Constitution of the United States, all, or any of which Articles, when ratified by three fourths of the said Legislatures, to be valid to all intents and purposes, as part of the said Constitution;

ARTICLES in addition to, and Amendment of the Constitution of the United States of America, proposed by Congress, and ratified by the Legislatures of the several States, pursuant to the fifth Article of the original Constitution. (Articles I through X are known as the Bill of Rights)

-

Article the first. .... After the first enumeration required by the first Article of the Constitution, there shall be one Representative for every thirty thousand, until the number shall amount to one hundred, after which, the proportion shall be so regulated by Congress, that there shall be not less than one hundred Representatives, nor less than one Representative for every forty thousand persons, until the number of Representatives shall amount to two hundred, after which the proportion shall be so regulated by Congress, that there shall not be less than two hundred Representatives, nor more than one Representative for every fifty thousand persons.

-

Article the second. .... No law, varying the compensation for the services of the Senators and Representatives, shall take effect, until an election of Representatives shall have intervened. see Amendment XXVII

Article [I]

Congress shall make no law respecting an establishment of religion, or prohibiting the free exercise thereof; or abridging the freedom of speech, or of the press; or the right of the people peaceably to assemble, and to petition the Government for a redress of grievances.

Article [II]

A well regulated Militia, being necessary to the security of a free State, the right of the people to keep and bear Arms, shall not be infringed.

Article [III]

No Soldier shall, in time of peace be quartered in any house, without the

consent of the Owner, nor in time of war, but in a manner to be prescribed by law.

Article [IV]

The right of the people to be secure in their persons, houses, papers, and effects, against unreasonable searches and seizures, shall not be violated, and no Warrants shall issue, but upon probable cause, supported by Oath or affirmation, and particularly describing the place to be searched, and the persons or things to be seized.

Article [V]

No person shall be held to answer for a capital, or otherwise infamous crime, unless on a presentment or indictment of a Grand Jury, except in cases arising in the land or naval forces, or in the Militia, when in actual service in time of War or public danger; nor shall any person be subject for the same offense to be twice put in jeopardy of life or limb; nor shall be compelled in any criminal case to be a witness against himself, nor be deprived of life, liberty, or property, without due process of law; nor shall private property be taken for public use, without just compensation.

Article [VI]

In all criminal prosecutions, the accused shall enjoy the right to a speedy and public trial, by an impartial jury of the State and district wherein the crime shall have been committed, which district shall have been previously ascertained by law, and to be informed of the nature and cause of the accusation; to be confronted with the witnesses against him; to have compulsory process for obtaining witnesses in his favor, and to have the Assistance of Counsel for his defense.

Article [VII]

In Suits at common law, where the value in controversy shall exceed twenty dollars, the right of trial by jury shall be preserved, and no fact tried by a jury, shall be otherwise re-examined in any Court of the United States, than according to the rules of the common law.

Article [VIII]

Excessive bail shall not be required, nor excessive fines imposed, nor cruel and unusual punishments inflicted.

Article [IX]

The enumeration in the Constitution, of certain rights, shall not be construed to deny or disparage others retained by the people.

Article [X]

The powers not delegated to the United States by the Constitution, nor prohibited by it to the States, are reserved to the States respectively, or to the people.

(end of the Bill of Rights)
[Article XI]

The Judicial power of the United States shall not be construed to extend to any suit in law or equity, commenced or prosecuted against one of the United States by Citizens of another State, or by Citizens or Subjects of any Foreign State.

[Article XII]

The Electors shall meet in their respective states, and vote by ballot for President and Vice-President, one of whom, at least, shall not be an inhabitant of the same state with themselves; they shall name in their ballots the person voted for as President, and in distinct ballots the person voted for as Vice-President, and they shall make distinct lists of all persons voted for as President, and of all persons voted for as Vice-President, and of the number of votes for each, which lists they shall sign and certify, and transmit sealed to the seat of the government of the United States, directed to the President of the Senate;--The President of the Senate shall, in the presence of the Senate and House of Representatives, open all the certificates and the votes shall then be counted;--The person having the greatest number of votes for President, shall be the President, if such number be a majority of the whole number of Electors appointed; and if no person have such majority, then from the persons having the highest numbers not exceeding three on the list of those voted for as President, the House of Representatives shall choose immediately, by ballot, the President. But in choosing the President, the votes shall be taken by states, the representation from each state having one vote; a quorum for this purpose shall consist of a member or members from two-thirds of the states, and a majority of all the states shall be necessary to a choice. And if the House of Representatives shall not choose a President whenever the right of choice shall devolve upon them, before the fourth day of March next following, then the Vice-President shall act as President, as in the case of the death or other constitutional disability of the President.14 --The person having the greatest number of votes as Vice-President, shall be the Vice-President, if such number be a majority of the whole number of Electors appointed, and if no person have a majority, then from the two highest numbers on the list, the Senate shall choose the Vice-President; a quorum for the purpose shall consist of two-thirds of the whole number of Senators, and a majority of the whole number shall be necessary to a choice. But no person constitutionally ineligible to the office of President shall be eligible to that of Vice-President of the United States.

Article XIII

Neither slavery nor involuntary servitude, except as a punishment for crime whereof the party shall have been duly convicted, shall exist within the United States, or any place subject to their jurisdiction.
Congress shall have power to enforce this article by appropriate legislation.

Article XIV

1: All persons born or naturalized in the United States, and subject to the jurisdiction thereof, are citizens of the United States and of the State wherein they reside. No State shall make or enforce any law which shall abridge the privileges or immunities of citizens of the United States; nor shall any State deprive any person of life, liberty, or property, without due process of law; nor deny to any person within its jurisdiction the equal protection of the laws.

2: Representatives shall be apportioned among the several States according to their respective numbers, counting the whole number of persons in each

State, excluding Indians not taxed. But when the right to vote at any election for the choice of electors for President and Vice President of the United States, Representatives in Congress, the Executive and Judicial officers of a State, or the members of the Legislature thereof, is denied to any of the male inhabitants of such State, being twenty-one years of age, and citizens of the United States, or in any way abridged, except for participation in rebellion, or other crime, the basis of representation therein shall be reduced in the proportion which the number of such male citizens shall bear to the whole number of male citizens twenty-one years of age in such State.

3: No person shall be a Senator or Representative in Congress, or elector of President and Vice President, or hold any office, civil or military, under the United States, or under any State, who, having previously taken an oath, as a member of Congress, or as an officer of the United States, or as a member of any State legislature, or as an executive or judicial officer of any State, to support the Constitution of the United States, shall have engaged in insurrection or rebellion against the same, or given aid or comfort to the enemies thereof. But Congress may by a vote of two-thirds of each House, remove such disability.

4: The validity of the public debt of the United States, authorized by law, including debts incurred for payment of pensions and bounties for services in suppressing insurrection or rebellion, shall not be questioned. But neither the United States nor any State shall assume or pay any debt or obligation incurred in aid of insurrection or rebellion against the United States, or any claim for the loss or emancipation of any slave; but all such debts, obligations and claims shall be held illegal and void.

5: The Congress shall have power to enforce, by appropriate legislation, the provisions of this article.

Article XV

The right of citizens of the United States to vote shall not be denied or abridged by the United States or by any State on account of race, color, or previous condition of servitude.

The Congress shall have power to enforce this article by appropriate legislation.

Article XVI

The Congress shall have power to lay and collect taxes on incomes, from whatever source derived, without apportionment among the several States, and without regard to any census or enumeration.

[Article XVII]

1: The Senate of the United States shall be composed of two Senators from each State, elected by the people thereof, for six years; and each Senator shall have one vote. The electors in each State shall have the qualifications requisite for electors of the most numerous branch of the State legislatures.

2: When vacancies happen in the representation of any State in the Senate, the executive authority of such State shall issue writs of election to fill such vacancies: Provided, That the legislature of any State may empower the executive thereof to make temporary appointments until the people fill the vacancies by election as the legislature may direct.

3: This amendment shall not be so construed as to affect the election or term of any Senator chosen before it becomes valid as part of the Constitution.

Article [XVIII]

1: After one year from the ratification of this article the manufacture, sale, or transportation of intoxicating liquors within, the importation thereof into, or the exportation thereof from the United States and all territory subject to the jurisdiction thereof for beverage purposes is hereby prohibited.

2: The Congress and the several States shall have concurrent power to enforce this article by appropriate legislation.

3: This article shall be inoperative unless it shall have been ratified as an amendment to the Constitution by the legislatures of the several States, as provided in the Constitution, within seven years from the date of the submission hereof to the States by the Congress.

Article [XIX]

The right of citizens of the United States to vote shall not be denied or abridged by the United States or by any State on account of sex.

Congress shall have power to enforce this article by appropriate legislation.

Article [XX]

1: The terms of the President and Vice President shall end at noon on the 20th day of January, and the terms of Senators and Representatives at noon on the 3d day of January, of the years in which such terms would have ended if this article had not been ratified; and the terms of their successors shall then begin.

2: The Congress shall assemble at least once in every year, and such meeting shall begin at noon on the 3d day of January, unless they shall by law appoint a different day.

3: If, at the time fixed for the beginning of the term of the President, the President elect shall have died, the Vice President elect shall become President. If a President shall not have been chosen before the time fixed for the beginning of his term, or if the President elect shall have failed to qualify, then the Vice President elect shall act as President until a President shall have qualified; and the Congress may by law provide for the case wherein neither a President elect nor a Vice President elect shall have qualified, declaring who shall then act as President, or the manner in which one who is to act shall be selected, and such person shall act accordingly until a President or Vice President shall have qualified.

4: The Congress may by law provide for the case of the death of any of the persons from whom the House of Representatives may choose a President whenever the right of choice shall have devolved upon them, and for the case of the death of any of the persons from whom the Senate may choose a Vice President whenever the right of choice shall have devolved upon them.

5: Sections 1 and 2 shall take effect on the 15th day of October following the ratification of this article.

6: This article shall be inoperative unless it shall have been ratified as an amendment to the Constitution by the legislatures of three-fourths of the several States within seven years from the date of its submission.

Article [XXI]

1: The eighteenth article of amendment to the Constitution of the United States is hereby repealed.

2: The transportation or importation into any State, Territory, or possession of the United States for delivery or use therein of intoxicating liquors, in violation of the laws thereof, is hereby prohibited.

3: This article shall be inoperative unless it shall have been ratified as an amendment to the Constitution by conventions in the several States, as provided in the Constitution, within seven years from the date of the submission hereof to the States by the Congress.

Amendment XXII

1: No person shall be elected to the office of the President more than twice, and no person who has held the office of President, or acted as President, for more than two years of a term to which some other person was elected President shall be elected to the office of the President more than once. But this article shall not apply to any person holding the office of President when this article was proposed by the Congress, and shall not prevent any person who may be holding the office of President, or acting as President, during the term within which this article becomes operative from holding the office of President or acting as President during the remainder of such term.

2: This article shall be inoperative unless it shall have been ratified as an amendment to the Constitution by the legislatures of three-fourths of the several states within seven years from the date of its submission to the states by the Congress.

Amendment XXIII

1: The District constituting the seat of government of the United States

shall appoint in such manner as the Congress may direct: A number of electors of President and Vice President equal to the whole number of Senators and Representatives in Congress to which the District would be entitled if it were a state, but in no event more than the least populous state; they shall be in addition to those appointed by the states, but they shall be considered, for the purposes of the election of President and Vice President, to be electors appointed by a state; and they shall meet in the District and perform such duties as provided by the twelfth article of amendment.

2: The Congress shall have power to enforce this article by appropriate legislation.

Amendment XXIV

1. The right of citizens of the United States to vote in any primary or other election for President or Vice President, for electors for President or Vice President, or for Senator or Representative in Congress, shall not be denied or abridged by the United States or any state by reason of failure to pay any poll tax or other tax.

2. The Congress shall have power to enforce this article by appropriate legislation.

Amendment XXV

1: In case of the removal of the President from office or of his death or resignation, the Vice President shall become President.

2: Whenever there is a vacancy in the office of the Vice President, the President shall nominate a Vice President who shall take office upon confirmation by a majority vote of both Houses of Congress.

3: Whenever the President transmits to the President pro tempore of the

Senate and the Speaker of the House of Representatives his written

declaration that he is unable to discharge the powers and duties of his office, and until he transmits to them a written declaration to the contrary, such powers and duties shall be discharged by the Vice President as Acting President.

4: Whenever the Vice President and a majority of either the principal officers of the executive departments or of such other body as Congress may by law provide, transmit to the President pro tempore of the Senate and the Speaker of the House of Representatives their written declaration that the President is unable to discharge the powers and duties of his office, the Vice President shall immediately assume the powers and duties of the office as Acting President.

Thereafter, when the President transmits to the President pro tempore of the Senate and the Speaker of the House of Representatives his written declaration that no inability exists, he shall resume the powers and duties of his office unless the Vice President and a majority of either the principal officers of the executive department or of such other body as Congress may by law provide, transmit within four days to the President pro tempore of the Senate and the Speaker of the House of Representatives their written declaration that the President is unable to discharge the powers and duties of his office. Thereupon Congress shall decide the issue, assembling within forty-eight hours for that purpose if not in session. If the Congress, within twenty-one days after receipt of the latter written declaration, or, if Congress is not in session, within twenty-one days after Congress is required to assemble, determines by two-thirds vote of both Houses that the President is unable to discharge the powers and duties of his office, the Vice President shall continue to discharge the same as Acting President; otherwise, the President shall resume the powers and duties of his office.

Amendment XXVI

1: The right of citizens of the United States, who are 18 years of age or older, to vote, shall not be denied or abridged by the United States or any state on account of age.

2: The Congress shall have the power to enforce this article by appropriate

legislation.

Amendment XXVII

No law varying the compensation for the services of the Senators and Representatives shall take effect until an election of Representatives shall have intervened.

NOW REMEMBER PEOPLE, you have these rights.....Why are you

NOT knowledgeable of them?

Keep them in your mind, at all times....

AND Remember, people died for this...knowledge you have now......

Remember this old man never gives up on anyone, esp. someone suffering from injustice, like I have....

If you have any questions or comments, please do not hesitate to get a hold of me at <u>usnavyveteran19682013@gmail.com</u>

God bless you and yours....Keep your faith, no matter what you believe in and let your path be always positive...

Blessings

Rev. Russell J. Young